The Great Asian
TSUNAMI

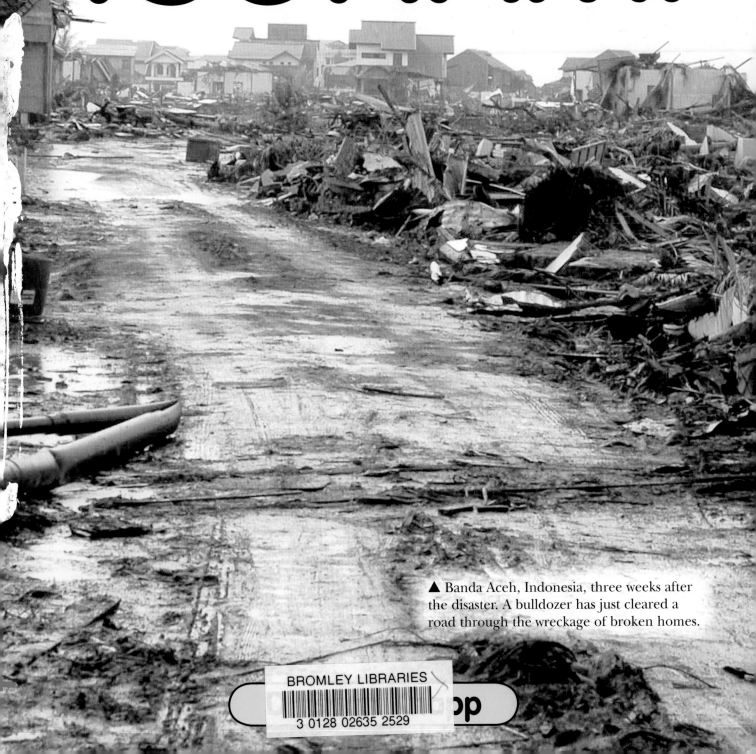

▲ Banda Aceh, Indonesia, three weeks after the disaster. A bulldozer has just cleared a road through the wreckage of broken homes.

◈ *Atlantic Europe Publishing*

First published in 2005 by
Atlantic Europe Publishing Company Ltd.

Author
Dr Brian Knapp, BSc, PhD

Art Director
Duncan McCrae, BSc

Senior Designer
Adele Humphries, BA, PGCE

Editors
Lisa Magloff, MA, and Gillian Gatehouse

Designed and produced by
EARTHSCAPE EDITIONS

Printed and bound in UK by
Halstan & Co., Ltd

**The Great Asian Tsunami
– Curriculum Visions**
**A CIP record for this book is
available from the British Library**
Paperback ISBN 1 86214 475 3
Hardback ISBN 1 86214 477 X

Illustrations
All illustrations by *David Woodroffe*,
except pages 14–15 *Tim Smith*.

Picture credits
All diagrams are copyright of Atlantic
Europe Publishing unless otherwise stated.
All photographs are by the US Navy, except
the following (c=centre t=top b=bottom
l=left r=right):

*Centre for Remote Imaging, Sensing and
Processing, National University of Singapore and
Space Imaging/IKONOS* 5tr, 5br; *Digital Globe/
Quickbird* 10tr.

Curriculum Visions

Curriculum Visions is a registered trademark of
Atlantic Europe Publishing Company Ltd.

More images
Our Picture Gallery CD contains even more captioned
photographs and some animated diagrams.

Other teaching resources
A Teacher's Guide containing classroom ideas,
activities and worksheets has been created to
accompany this book.

There's more on-line
There is more about our other Curriculum Visions
resources and a wealth of supporting information at
our dedicated web site:

www.CurriculumVisions.com

Glossary words
There is a glossary and index on page 24.
Glossary terms are shown in the text by using **CAPITALS**.

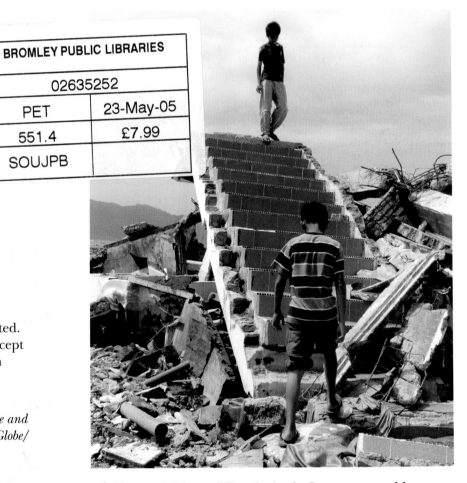

▲ **Young children of Banda Aceh, Sumatra, stand by
the only piece that remains of their home after the
devastating tsunami (sometimes known as a** TIDAL WAVE**)
hit their town on 26 December 2004.**

Contents

▲ In the wake of the 2004 tsunami, medical teams rush in to treat the injured in Aceh, Indonesia.

Most damaging tsunamis in history

Those affecting Indonesia are highlighted in yellow.

Deaths	Year	Location
250,000+	2004	Indian Ocean off North West Sumatra: 12 Indian Ocean Countries
40,000	1782	South China Sea
36,500	1883	South Java Sea (Krakatoa Volcano)
30,000	1707	Tokaido-nankaido, Japan
26,360	1896	Sanriku, Japan
25,674	1868	North Chile
15,030	1792	South West Kyushu Island, Japan
13,486	1771	Ryukyu Trench
8,000	1976	Moro Gulf, Philippines
5,233	1703	Tokaido-kashima, Japan
5,000	1605	Nankaido, Japan
5,000	1611	Sanriku, Japan
3,800	1746	Lima, Peru
3,620	1899	Banda Sea, Indonesia
3,000	1692	Jamaica
3,000	1854	Nankaido, Japan
3,000	1933	Sanriku, Japan
2,243	1674	Banda Sea, Indonesia
2,182	1998	Papua New Guinea
2,144	1923	Tokaido, Japan
2,000	1570	Chile
1,997	1946	Nankaido, Japan
1,700	1766	Sanriku, Japan
119	1964	Alaska, USA

(source: NOAA)

The Great Asian Tsunami

One of the largest ever natural disasters struck twelve countries on 26 December 2004. By the time it was all over, it had killed about a quarter of a million people and left over five million homeless.

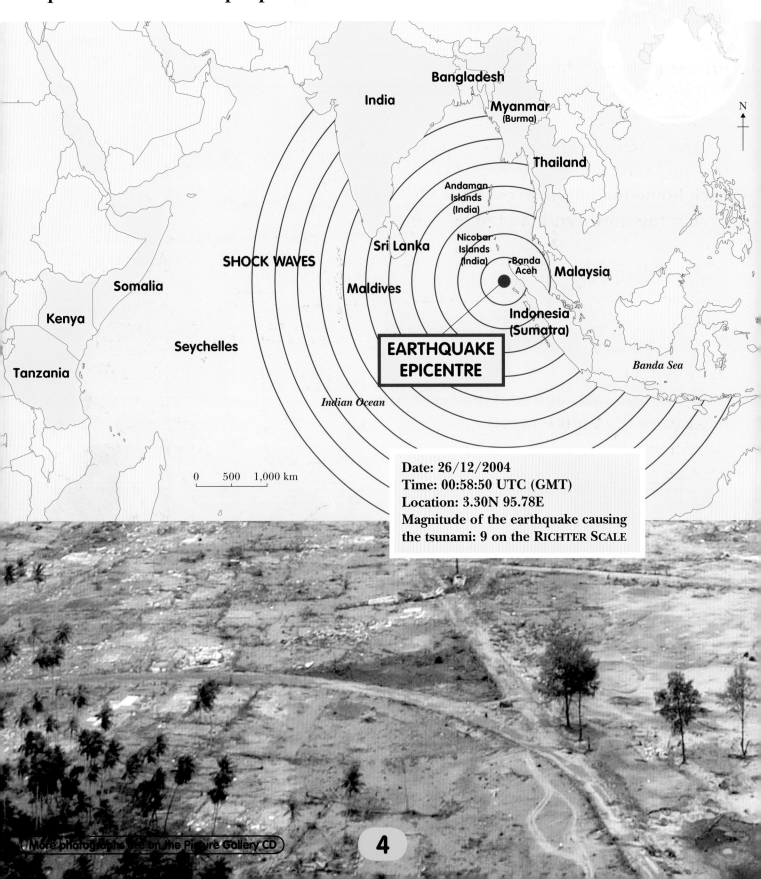

N

Bangladesh

India

Myanmar
(Burma)

Thailand

Andaman
Islands
(India)

Nicobar
Islands
(India)

Banda
Aceh

Malaysia

SHOCK WAVES

Sri Lanka

Somalia

Maldives

Indonesia
(Sumatra)

Kenya

Seychelles

Banda Sea

Tanzania

EARTHQUAKE
EPICENTRE

Indian Ocean

0   500   1,000 km

Date: 26/12/2004
Time: 00:58:50 UTC (GMT)
Location: 3.30N 95.78E
Magnitude of the earthquake causing
the tsunami: 9 on the RICHTER SCALE

More photographs are on the Picture Gallery CD

It was 07:58:52 AM in the eastern Indian Ocean near Indonesia…

In Britain, Boxing Day was just an hour old. In Australia, people were eating lunch. In the USA, the last of the Christmas Day celebrations were still in full swing. To all of these people life seemed good. Many of their friends and relatives were on holiday in the coastal resorts around the Indian Ocean. They had gone to soak up the sun and warmth of the tropics. People back home toasted their good health.

Off the northern island of Sumatra, Indonesia, local fishermen had just set off for a day in their fishing boats, and the coastal towns were already a-buzz with life.

In the coastal resorts of Thailand the foreign tourists were just getting ready for breakfast and looking forward to another day on the beach.

All in all, it was going to be just another lazy, sunny day…

▲▼ ② These pictures show the same part of Lhoknga, Indonesia, before and immediately after the tsunami. Tropical forest is green. There is almost no green in the bottom picture and only white shadows where once there were red-roofed houses.

(source: Centre for Remote Imaging, Sensing and Processing, National University of Singapore and Space Imaging/IKONOS)

◀ ① The coastal town of Banda Aceh in northern Indonesia caught the brunt of the tsunami. Waves here were over 10 m high and arrived within minutes of the nearby quake. The coastal part of the town was completely destroyed. What you see was once houses and shops. The road pattern is all that remains.

…Until, at precisely 07:58:53, a part of the sea floor just off Sumatra snapped. It was the size of England (see page 9).

The ocean bed, and the 1,200 m of water above it, were instantaneously heaved about 10 m upwards like a giant fist punching from the Earth. No one witnessed this. It was far out to sea.

But in the world's EARTHQUAKE recording stations around the Pacific Ocean (where tsunamis are much more common) alarm bells were ringing. Those on duty knew that their machines, thousands of kilometres from where the earthquake had happened, were recording something that had occurred only three times previously in the last century – a magnitude 9 earthquake.

Immediately they tried to locate the source of the earthquake and its depth. Soon they knew it was just 33 km below the floor of the Indian Ocean. They held their breath. They knew what this could mean – a TSUNAMI, or giant wave – but they could do nothing…

In Indonesia the first shock waves from this large underwater earthquake reached the towns and cities of the northern island of Sumatra. The ground shook and some houses collapsed.

◄ ③ In Banda Aceh, very few buildings near the coast survived. All around are the ruins of people's homes and shops. Many were made of wood frames with tin roofs, but even poorly-constructed brick buildings were destroyed. This mosque was one of the survivors because it was so sturdily built.

People in the coastal town of Banda Aceh rushed from their homes and began to see if anyone was hurt and to look at the damage.

Out in the ocean a ripple spread silently outwards. It was less than a metre high but it was a hundred kilometres wide and moving at over 600 kilometres an hour – the speed of an airliner.

A few minutes later the ripple (which contained billions of tonnes of water) ran silently onto the shallow Sumatran coast. It touched bottom and as it rubbed against the sea bed it was slowed down to the speed of a car. But the same volume of water was still on the move, so the wave changed shape, rearing up into a monster which, on the Sumatran coast, was as high as a house.

People stopped to look. First they saw the sea level fall in a matter of seconds. Children on the coast ran onto the beaches to pick up the fish left floundering. But almost immediately a wave could be seen rushing in towards them, growing taller and taller as it approached. It was the last thing they ever saw. They had no time to escape. Within seconds their towns were no more than flattened matchwood (picture ①).

It was just the start of one of the world's worst international natural disasters (pictures ②, ③, ④ and ⑤).

▲ ④ Boats were torn from their moorings and thrown on to the land to be broken up and their cargoes were scattered or dumped in among buildings.

◄ ⑤ When the waters subsided, bodies were found among the debris. They had to be collected, put into body bags, then buried – a distressing task for the survivors.

Weblink: www.CurriculumVisions.com/tsunami

Why did it happen?

The tsunami was caused by an earthquake just below the sea floor off the coast of Indonesia.

The deaths of more than 250,000 people were caused by nature. This was nothing unusual in the four billion years of Earth's history. During this time the Earth has developed a thin, solid, brittle **CRUST**. It is the rock we live on. But below it lies material that is hot and continually on the move (see picture ①). This is the source of **EARTHQUAKES** and **VOLCANOES** which in turn can cause **TSUNAMIS**.

The layer below the crust is called the **MANTLE**. It is like a sticky, hot plastic. It moves at just a few centimetres a year. But it is so powerful that it simply drags the crust with it. The crust is brittle and cannot move easily, so stresses build up as the mantle tugs at the crust. Eventually the crust gives way and snaps.

▼ ① The world's crust is split into PLATES. The edges of splitting plates are shown by the purple lines, whereas the colliding plates are shown by orange lines. The way the plates move is shown by blue arrows, and the places where earthquakes happen is shown by red dots. The earthquake location that caused the Great Asian Tsunami is marked.

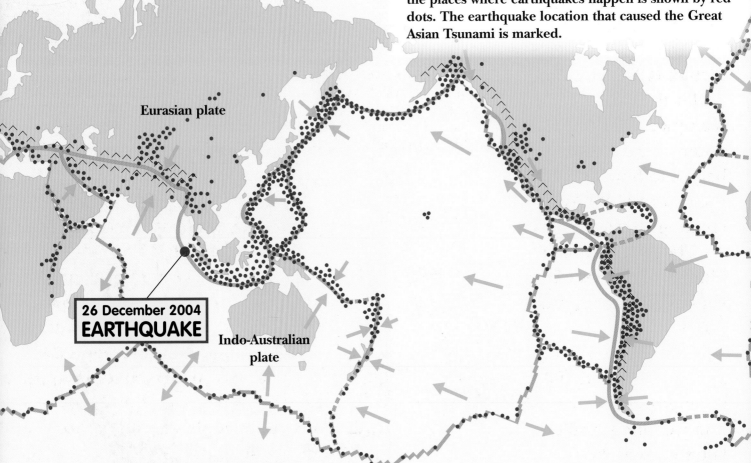

Eurasian plate

26 December 2004
EARTHQUAKE

Indo-Australian plate

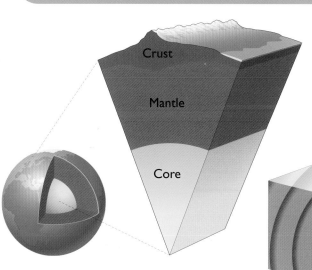

◀▼ ② These diagrams show how the Earth is divided into layers (left) and how movements of the crust cause earthquakes (below).

▼ ③ Earthquakes form at places where plates collide. They are often the same places as where volcanoes erupt. Sumatra, Indonesia, is a volcanic island located where the Indian plate collides, and is carried under the Australian plate.

Movement due to earthquake

EPICENTRE

Shock waves

The snap sends out shock waves and the shock waves produce an earthquake (see pictures ② and ③).

At the same time, the snapping rock moves up or down. Huge slabs of crust the size of England can move within seconds (see picture ④). If this happens under the ocean, it lifts the sea upwards into a dome of water. The sea water then begins to flow away from the centre of this dome, creating a series of waves.

The waves contain billions of tonnes of water. Yet out at sea they are not noticeable. A typical tsunami is half a metre high and 100 kilometres wide, but it moves at over 600 kilometres an hour.

▼ ④ The size of the slab of ocean crust that was pushed up 10 m was about the same size as England (shown for scale only).

The energy in this water is beyond imagination. Throw a bottle of water (a litre weighs a kilo) at a chair and you will knock it over. Then try to picture the result of billions of tonnes of water moving 100 times faster.

In the ocean the tsunami is hardly noticed. But as soon as the waves reach the coast all of the energy stored in the water is used in smashing up the land, plants, buildings and people who might be close to the sea.

Weblink: www.CurriculumVisions.com/tsunami

Countries affected
Bangladesh
India (including Andaman and Nicobar islands)
Indonesia
Kenya
Malaysia
Maldives
Myanmar (Burma)
Seychelles
Somalia
Sri Lanka
Tanzania
Thailand

Why were so many countries affected?

The tsunami spread out in the shape of a giant lozenge. It reached nearby shores in a few minutes, but took eight hours to cross the Indian Ocean and even longer to reach Africa. Even after all that distance it had the ability to kill (picture ①).

▲ ① Many parts of Sri Lanka, India and even Africa experienced a tsunami severe enough to cause great coastal flooding. In this picture of part of the Sri Lankan coast you see the flood waters rushing back into the Indian Ocean just a little while after the tsunami pushed ashore (see story page 14).

(source: DigitalGlobe)

Stages of a tsunami *(source NOAA)*

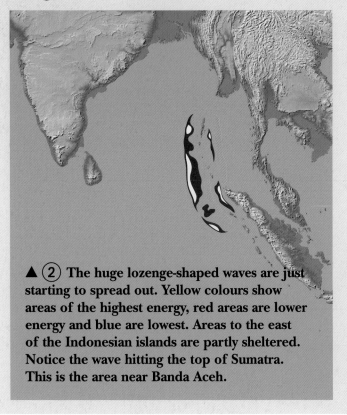

▲ ② The huge lozenge-shaped waves are just starting to spread out. Yellow colours show areas of the highest energy, red areas are lower energy and blue are lowest. Areas to the east of the Indonesian islands are partly sheltered. Notice the wave hitting the top of Sumatra. This is the area near Banda Aceh.

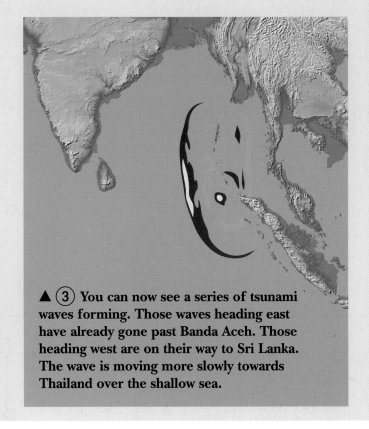

▲ ③ You can now see a series of tsunami waves forming. Those waves heading east have already gone past Banda Aceh. Those heading west are on their way to Sri Lanka. The wave is moving more slowly towards Thailand over the shallow sea.

More photographs are on the Picture Gallery CD

A tsunami is triggered by an earthquake under water. The result is very different from when an earthquake occurs on land.

To understand this, imagine tapping a tray of sand from underneath. This will be our model of an earthquake on land. The sand close to the tapping shakes, a little sand moves, but it all happens close to the 'earthquake'.

In the sea things are different. Tap a tray of water from underneath and the ripples spread out smoothly until they reach the edges of the tray. Then they change to waves that lap on the 'shores'. This is because very little energy has been soaked up by the water as the ripple moves through it.

Now look at pictures ② to ⑤. They show a model of what may have happened.

The ground that heaved up was lozenge-shaped and so the wave that spread out from this was also lozenge-shaped. Because the wave spread out without losing much energy, many places were affected and the number of countries that suffered disaster was large. The tsunami affected countries, like those in Africa, thousands of kilometres away from the source of the tsunami.

However, people close to the **EPICENTRE** received a much stronger tsunami than those further away, so the destruction was much worse in some countries than others.

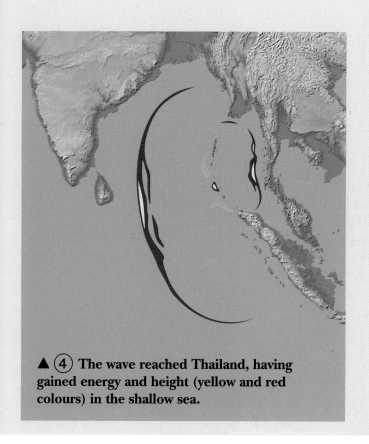

▲ ④ The wave reached Thailand, having gained energy and height (yellow and red colours) in the shallow sea.

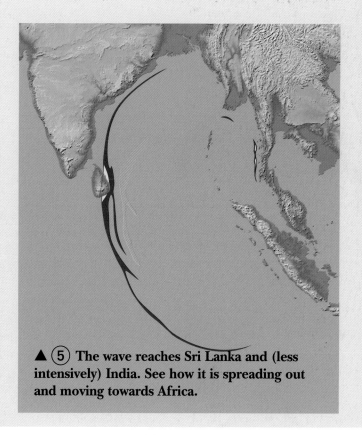

▲ ⑤ The wave reaches Sri Lanka and (less intensively) India. See how it is spreading out and moving towards Africa.

The wave of death

The tsunami rushed across the Indian Ocean at the speed of an airliner. Then it slowed down, reared up and crashed onto the shore.

The ocean is deep. But it becomes shallower towards the coast. So as waves move onto the coast they 'touch bottom' and are slowed down by friction with the ocean floor. The volume of the moving water can no longer be contained in the depth of the ocean and so it begins to rear up.

All seaside waves behave this way. This is why, for example, **BREAKERS** only occur at the coast, not out at sea. Essentially, the tsunami wave behaved the same way, like a gigantic wave. Such huge waves do not have a curling crest, but are more like a wall of water. When they reach the shore the water simply pushes in over the coast.

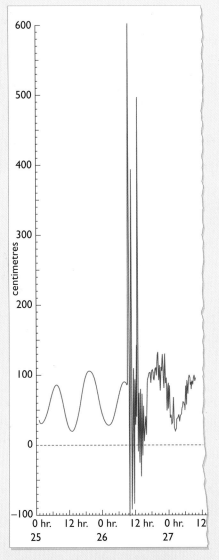

▲ ① The heights of tides are recorded by gauges around the Indian Ocean. Normally the ocean level rises and falls in a regular way (see left) but when the tsunami struck, most tide gauges went off their scales. Notice that several waves were recorded. This diagram is a composite of several gauges. Those in places where there were very high waves were destroyed and so we can only guess at what they might have shown.

A tsunami is not made of a single wave. Think of the many ripples made by a pebble thrown into a pond. A tsunami is also made up of many waves (picture ①).

The speed and mass of the water (its momentum) drove the wave inland (pictures ② to ⑦). On flat coastal plains it moved like a giant bulldozer for several kilometres before its energy was spent. As the water destroyed buildings, it carried the debris with it, and this turned the wave into a battering ram of mud, bricks, timber, cars and roofing sheets. No one caught in this frightful flow could hope to escape.

Carrying debris used up energy, and so the waves finally came to rest. Then the waves flowed back out again, this time as a flood of water and debris that tore at any remaining objects, pulling trees, houses, and people back out to the sea…

…And then it was over. But the struggle for human survival was just beginning…

Stages of the tsunami disaster

▼ ② It is calm before the tsunami, but out in the ocean the tsunami waves are approaching at the speed of a jet airliner.

▼ ③ The sea level falls rapidly.

▼ ④ The first tsunami wave runs in at the speed of a car.

▼ ⑤ The momentum of the water bulldozes all but the strongest of buildings into rubble.

▼ ⑥ The wave energy is spent. The land is flooded. Now the flood water rushes back to sea.

▼ ⑦ When the flood is gone, the wreckage is revealed.

Weblink: www.CurriculumVisions.com/tsunami

They ran for their lives

Eyewitnesses tell many dramatic stories of what it was like to experience the tsunami.

There is no better way to understand what the tsunami was like than to read about the experiences of eyewitnesses. Here are just a few:

In Penang, Malaysia, a group of Japanese tourists were in a hotel when they felt the earthquake tremors. Earthquakes are common in Japan and so the Japanese know all about tsunamis (the word tsunami is Japanese for big wave). They had been taught that you do not want to be close to the sea after an earthquake just in case it produces a tsunami. So they rushed to the nearby hills and survived.

On Phuket Island, Thailand, an English girl on holiday with her family remembered what she learned about tsunamis in her geography lessons. When the tsunami began, she knew what it meant and shouted at people to flee. She saved countless lives.

Off the coast of Banda Aceh, Indonesian fishermen in rowing boats were carried far out to sea by the waves. They spent eight days with no food or water until finally drifting close to the Andaman Islands where they were rescued. But their home town was gone.

▶ Here is a more detailed story. It belongs to the children who live in an orphanage near a small coastal village in the south east of India. Their area was not as badly affected as some others, and so most lived to tell the tale. But for them it was still a great and fearful disaster. Here is an edited account of a long e-mail sent just a few days after the disaster.

On Phuket, a local family were playing on the beach when they saw the tsunami. The mother picked up one of her children and rushed inland. The father picked up the second, but he paused to look back. In that split second of delay they were washed inland by the tsunami. The child managed to cling on to a house and was saved, but no trace was found of the father.

◀ An artist's impression of the first wave striking the coast and its impact on the many flimsily-built houses.

"The Christmas celebration went very well. We had fixed the date to go to the sea shore on the morning of the 26th Dec and Shalem Raju took the children that morning. Some children were just watching, while others bathed in the sea.

Just before 9 AM Shalem Raju asked the children to go back home because their time was up.

Suddenly, at 9 AM, the huge sea wave rose up some 10 m and rushed out strongly. Everyone at the sea shore ran with great fear. After 15 minutes, Shalem Raju could not find two children. With great fear he went to the sea and was searching for them, but he asked the other children not to come with him.

Suddenly another wave rose up and rushed onto the shore. One bus, two motor vehicles and a jeep were drowned in the sea, and those who were searching for others ran for their lives again with so much fearful hearts.

Then a third wave came. Shalem Raju, like the others, was now too fearful to go to the sea and all the searchers left the beach.

After one hour Shalem Raju sent all the children home and started to search for the two missing girls. After two hours he found the dead body of one of them a distance of one kilometre from the sea.

He was confused and did not know what to do and came for more help. With another person he searched for the other missing girl but could not find her.

None of the children can now sleep in the home.

All the nearby villagers fled to the town and some small houses (made of wood and zinc sheets) were destroyed.

In the nearby village five women, two men and four children died."

Please help!

Once the tsunami was over, millions of people were without shelter, food or clean water. Here is what it might have been like if you had been there.

▲ ① Lost and bewildered, this boy stands among the wreckage of his town a couple of days after the disaster.

Imagine… It is midday, local time in Banda Aceh, Indonesia, just a few hours after the tsunami has struck.

You are sitting on a pile of wood (picture ①). As far as you can see there is nothing but destruction. Lakes of muddy sea water are everywhere. You have no idea where your family are, or even whether they are alive or dead. You are in shock from having been battered by the giant wave, and from clinging to a tree until the floodwater went away. Now it is hot, and you are thirsty.

Unknown to you, all around the world people and governments are swinging into action, offering aid and assistance. The world's press is screaming about the disaster, and ordinary people are wondering about their friends and loved ones, and asking how they can help. Everyone is shocked. Most people do not even know what a tsunami is.

More photographs are on the Picture Gallery CD

But you do not know any of this. The people around you cannot help. They are just as shocked and lost as you are. The local emergency services in your area have been destroyed. You must wait for the government or international aid organisations to arrive…

As time goes by, you may wonder why no one is arriving. Because communication lines are down and roads are washed away, it takes some time for governments to realise the scale of the disaster and that they are overwhelmed and need outside help.

Those with experience of disasters know that emergency medical teams and clean water are the first priorities (picture ②). But first they must get trucks filled and the supplies onto planes, and the planes must be chartered. Suitable working airfields for cargo planes must be found, and they must get permission to land and operate. It all takes time.…

▼ ② **All over the world people are packing up essential items such as bottled water.**

It is the next day. No one has come. You are still waiting for help and water…

The planes take off, but it takes twelve hours to reach Banda Aceh. Once there, the aid cannot be distributed because there are no roads left. Big helicopters are needed, but the only people with big enough helicopters are the military.

Military from countries around the world begin sending teams to see what is needed, find landing sites and prepare for relief…

Evening comes. You are thirstier than ever. All around is muddy water. You start to look for food and water among the destroyed buildings: tins, bottles, anything…

It is the next day. You hear a helicopter come over the horizon, sweeping low, looking for survivors. It finds a clear piece of road to land on and someone jumps out, holding a bottle of water for you (picture ③).

You are saved.

▶ ③ **Help arrives from the air.**

Once assistance arrives

In order to be effective, emergency relief services must be well organised. They can only do this once they know the scale of the problem.

World assistance was planned from the first minute people learned of the disaster. It was planned on the experience of previous disasters. But even so, it is hard, at first, to know what you are dealing with. For example, the numbers first reported dead were just 11,000. But as more became known, the total was raised to 24,000, then 49,000, then 80,000, then 119,000, then 160,000 and finally to more than 250,000.

▼ (1) **The situation near Banda Aceh, Indonesia. The disaster affected a strip of Indonesia's coast over 800 km long.**

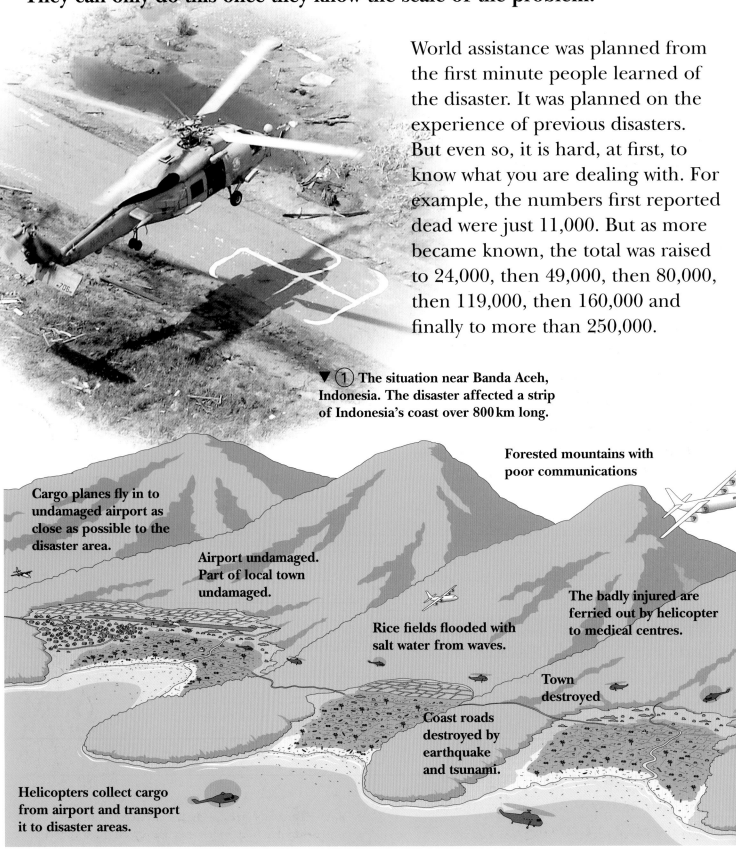

Forested mountains with poor communications

Cargo planes fly in to undamaged airport as close as possible to the disaster area.

Airport undamaged. Part of local town undamaged.

Rice fields flooded with salt water from waves.

The badly injured are ferried out by helicopter to medical centres.

Town destroyed

Coast roads destroyed by earthquake and tsunami.

Helicopters collect cargo from airport and transport it to disaster areas.

More photographs are on the Picture Gallery CD

▲ ② Aid workers and military personnel getting badly injured people into a helicopter. They were then air-lifted to the nearest hospital.

◄ ③ The navy brings in supplies to whatever patch of land they can land on.

▲ ④ Trucks, bulldozers and other essential items arrive by landing craft because the port has been destroyed.

It also took days before it was clear that the total number of homeless was five and a half million.

It is also important to know which places are most severely affected, and which areas can cope with little outside help. India and Thailand, for example, said they could mainly help themselves, but harder hit Sri Lanka and Indonesia knew the disaster was too much for them. So the biggest air effort went to Sri Lanka and Indonesia (picture ①).

This could not be done in seconds. Even by using the military, and especially its helicopters, it took more than a week before outlying areas were reached, injured people treated, food and water delivered and help given to those who had lost loved ones – such was the scale of the disaster (pictures ②, ③ and ④).

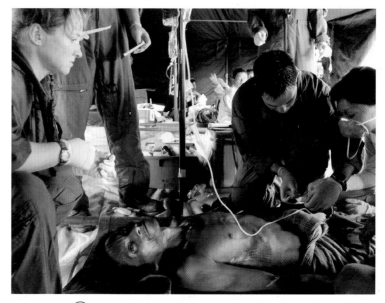

▲ ⑤ Tents are set up to give shelter to the wounded while they are helped by emergency medical teams.

The long road to recovery

At first the world was in shock. But gradually assistance arrived and people were cared for. Then it was necessary to begin to plan the long road to recovery.

Disasters on a massive scale can only be coped with by planning and understanding.

The first few hours and days are a scramble to help those who have been stricken. This is a dramatic time. But disasters soon turn from drama into drudgery as the long, less glamorous – but vital – task of rebuilding begins. Let's look at how this change happens, calling the two parts of recovery phase one and phase two.

Phase one

In phase one the military and aid agencies rush in as much emergency supplies as they can (pictures ① and ③). First water, with medicines. Then food, temporary shelters and toilets (picture ②). Bodies are buried as quickly as possible.

▶ ② Digging latrines is one of the less glamorous, but essential tasks.

▼ ① At first, keeping people alive is the most important priority. Desperate people scramble to get food for their families.

▲ ③ Collecting clothes and other basic items that stricken people will need.

Journalists soon arrive to tell the world (picture ④). As they send back their pictures and stories of horror, people around the world reach for the phone to send in donations. This is vital, because the aid agencies will have already spent much of their reserve money on shipping out supplies in the first few hours and they need more money to carry on the job (picture ⑤).

▲ ④ Well-known journalists broadcast live to the world, emphasising the scale of the disaster. This helps to show people why they should donate money.

▶ ⑤ People from overseas aid agencies talk with local organisers to think through the best ways of providing help.

Weblink: www.CurriculumVisions.com/tsunami

Within a few days, important government officials arrive (picture ⑥). It's better if those with the purse strings can get some idea of what is happening, so they understand better what their staff on the ground tell them over the coming weeks.

▲ ⑥ Senior government officials arrive to hear first hand what is needed.

In the tsunami disaster phase one lasted about three weeks.

Phase two

Phase one and phase two overlap. But you can tell when phase two is taking over because the world news turns elsewhere.

In phase two, unnoticed and hardly reported, governments send in organisers, people who can start to get bulldozers clearing roads, buy in timber and zinc sheeting to make new homes, and so on. They replace the military and begin the long haul to recovery (pictures ⑦ to ⑨).

▼ ⑦ Before people can return to damaged homes or rebuild on destroyed sites, important services need to be in place. Here a water pump is being put back into operation. The wreckage of Banda Aceh can be seen in the background.

Even though their faces are never shown on the news, their job is every bit as vital as those who were there in phase one. Everybody's help is needed, not just for a few days, but for years to come.

As more time goes by and people start to rebuild their lives, they will need help to plant new crops, build new homes and shops and to find new jobs. Many people will also need help in coming to terms with their tragic loss.

Gradually, as the weeks pass, you start to see pictures of smiling faces once again. Such is the amazing ability of people to pick themselves up and carry on with their lives.

In conclusion…

The Great Asian tsunami was a disaster on a massive scale. The fact that so many people were helped, and so few died from disease, is a tribute to the planning that was in place based on knowledge from previous disasters.

From this tragedy the lesson is learned again: we must be prepared for disasters, and that disasters cross country boundaries. It will be more so in the future. We must be ready.

▶ ⑨ **With pride and grace, this Indonesian woman clasps bottles of water as she begins to rebuild her shattered life.**

◀ ⑧ **Bringing in generators to get electric power going again.**

Glossary

BREAKER A wave that reaches the coast and then rises steeply, so that the leading edge of the wave develops foam.

CRUST The outermost layer of the Earth, typically 5 km thick under the oceans and 50 to 100 km thick under continents.

EARTHQUAKE Shaking of the Earth's surface caused by a sudden movement of rock within the Earth.

EPICENTRE The place on the ground surface immediately above the focus of an earthquake.

MANTLE The layer of the Earth between the crust and the core. It is approximately 3,000 km thick and is the largest of the Earth's major layers.

PLATE One of the great slabs of the outer part of the Earth. Plates cover the whole of the Earth's surface. The Earth's plates are separated by narrow zones of volcanic and earthquake activity.

RICHTER SCALE A system used to measure the strength of an earthquake. The scale measures the energy of the earthquake, not its effect on people. The scale was developed by Charles Richter, an American, in 1935. Each number on the scale is 10 times bigger or smaller than its neighbour. So a (large) magnitude 6 earthquake has ten times the energy of a magnitude 5. This is why a magnitude 6 causes far more vibration than a magnitude 5.

A magnitude 9 earthquake, such as the one described in this book, is a thousand times (3 Richter units) bigger than a magnitude 6. Magnitude 9 earthquakes are very rare and almost always cause disasters.

TIDAL WAVE An unusually large wave at high water resulting from natural movements of the tide. Also popularly, but inaccurately, applied to a giant destructive wave cause by an earthquake, the correct term for which is a tsunami.

TSUNAMI From the Japanese, meaning big wave. A large scale ocean wave or series of giant waves which are caused by an earthquake below an ocean floor. A tsunami travels at speeds of 600 to 800 kph and contains enough energy to travel right across oceans and even from one ocean to another. They are very low, broad waves in the open ocean (half a metre high and 100 km wide), but change speed and shape as they reach the coast, creating waves that can be as much as 15 m high. Their momentum can destroy and flood low-lying areas for several kilometres inland.

VOLCANO (i) A mountain produced by many eruptions of lava and ash. (ii) An opening in the Earth's surface through which lava and ash can erupt.

Index